Double Your Covers: Restaurant Marketing Made Simple

Rob McNicoll, MBA

Copper Monkey Consulting Ltd
Suite 6a Wessex House
St Leonard's Road
Bournemouth
Dorset
UK
BH8 8QS

Ordering Information:

Quantity sales. Special discounts are available on quantity purchases by corporations, associations, and others. For details, contact the publisher at the address above.

ISBN:1543127614
ISBN-13:978-1543127614

DEDICATION

To Joyce and Ava... my support and inspiration.

PAGE INTENTIONALLY LEFT BLANK

CONTENTS

- How can I bring customers into my restaurant night after night?
- What is the best way to get NEW customers?
- What is the best way to get EXISTING customers to keep coming back?

- What FREE ways are there for getting new customers using the internet?
- YOUR WEBSITE: Is my website really that important?
- ONLINE BUSINESS PAGES: How do I set up my Online Business Pages to get customers?
- SOCIAL MEDIA: Can social media really help with increasing my covers?
- ONLINE REVIEW SITES: How important are review sites, and how can I get reviews (even negative ones) to work for me?

- How do I use the internet to advertise my restaurant?
- How much should I be spending on Advertising?

ABOUT THE AUTHOR

Rob McNicoll is an internationally recognized Marketing Consultant, Speaker and Restaurant Marketing Specialist.

Over the past decade he has helped businesses across multiple sectors grow their businesses by over £21.9 million in additional revenues can counting,

In early 2016 Rob made the decision to focus his efforts in the hospitality and food service sector, and launched his flagship website **www.TheRestaurantMarketer.com**. The site has gone on to help 1000s of restaurant owners market their business more effectively.

On a day to day basis, Rob and his team work personally with multiple private clients, while continuing to develop a suite of targeted learning materials for the Restaurant sector to help them grow their businesses.

ROB MCNICOLL

2

INTRODUCTION
Double Your Covers – Restaurant Marketing Made Simple

This book has been written to address 3 concerns I hear daily within our community:

- "Restaurant Marketing is Hard"
- "Restaurant Marketing Takes Lots of Time"
- "Advertising Your Restaurant Doesn't Work"

Well I'm here to tell you that each one of this is wrong... and at the same time right.

Let me explain.

The reason most of us find marketing our Restaurant both difficult and time consuming is that we are Restaurateurs, not Marketers. This means there is a stack of guess work involved and, even worse, we end up copying what every other restaurant is doing, which makes it nearly impossible for our potential customers to tell us apart from the competition.

With this in mind we spend hours and hours trying to create adverts that don't bring in the amount of new customers we were expecting, which leads us onto the assumption that "Advertising Doesn't Work".

Here's the simple truth... and I want you to really take this to heart.

It's NOT your fault

Ask any marketer to swap roles with you, and they'd fall flat on their face within minutes of service starting, so how can you be expected to do what they do?

Actually... you can... and...

- It isn't difficult
- It isn't massively time consuming
- It works

And that's what this book is going to show you – a step by step approach to fill your restaurant day after day, <u>consistently</u>.

I'm going to teach why you only really need to focus on 2 main things when it comes to marketing, and then I'll show you some techniques you can start applying today to see results.

While this book aims to provide a comprehensive overview, we're always coming up with new strategies and effective real world techniques, so once you've finished reading this, head over to our website to check out even more resources:

www.TheRestaurantMarketer.com

CHAPTER ONE

Getting Customers

How can I bring customers into my restaurant night after night?

The methods you need to use are straightforward, and fall under two main areas of focus. You are probably already putting some degree of effort into one or both of these areas, but in the following chapters I am going to show you how to work smarter, not necessarily harder.

Quite simply, the first area of focus is getting new customers in, and the second is getting your existing customers to keep coming back for more. I understand that without knowing exactly how to do it, the task can seem quite daunting.

I remember when I was young, one Christmas my Mum and Dad gave me a paint by numbers painting – it was of a tiger I seem to remember. I sat down and painted little bits following the instructions of 1, 2, 3 for different colours, and by the time I finished it I had a pretty decent piece of art which was well beyond my young years.

Getting new customers into your restaurant and getting existing ones to come back is much the same thing: if you have a structured way of doing it, it actually becomes quite simple to do.

What is the best way to get NEW customers?

There are four ways you can get new customers into your business. The first is by attracting them online, using the internet. The second is offline: using newspapers, radio or TV advertising, or what's known as "Guerrilla Marketing" which we'll go into a bit later. The third is footfall: people wandering past your restaurant and deciding to come in. The fourth and final way is through recommendations and word of mouth.

| Online | Offline | Footfall | Word of Mouth |

What is the best way to get EXISTING customers to keep coming back?

Again, there are four methods to concentrate on when looking to get customers to keep coming back. The first one is that you need to capture their information, either on your website or when they're in your restaurant enjoying your food. The second method is to follow up regularly, in a non-intrusive way. The third is creating special customer events. Lastly, the fourth is creating customer-only offers - for example creating a loyalty program for your existing customers.

| Capture Information | Follow Up | Special Events | Loyalty Program |

Key Points:

GET NEW CUSTOMERS USING

* Online
* Offline
* Footfall
*Word of mouth

GET REPEAT CUSTOMERS BY

* Capturing information
* Following up regularly
* Customer events
* Customer-only offers

CHAPTER TWO

Free Online Advertising

What FREE ways are there for getting new customers using the internet?

There are a few powerful online opportunities which you can use to get new customers, without spending any money. Those are: your existing website; your online business pages; effective use of social media and finally, review websites.

YOUR WEBSITE: Is my website really that important?

Absolutely. Your website is arguably the most important asset you have online, bar your customer reviews.

Now, you have to think about your website as an online version of your business. If your website looks shoddy, old or outdated, it will drive away potential customers who have never been to your restaurant.

It's *absolutely critical* that you make it as close to an online version of your restaurant as possible, and make it look modern and professional.

The other thing to watch out for is not having a website at all, and then relying on a Facebook page to be the "Face" of your business online. We're seeing more and more example of this, and it's NEVER a good idea.

On the following page we'll show you an example of good design and bad design taken from real world websites (we've blurred out the names to be fair to the guilty party!)

Not a good site – looks a bit "thrown" together, although there are some good elements with the contact number, opening times and address being prominent.

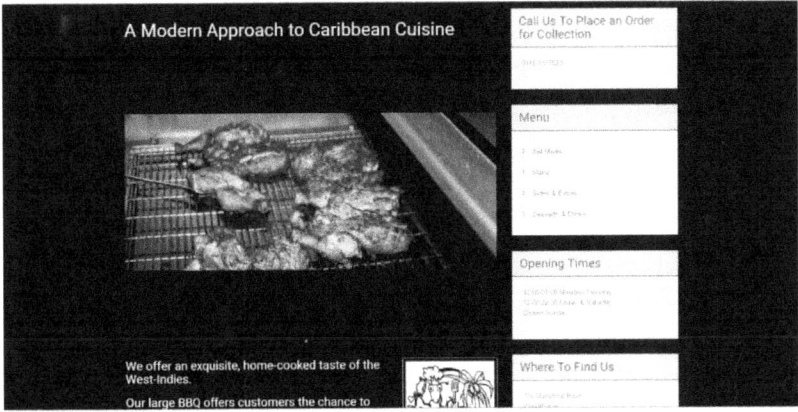

Here's a better example with nice imagery, clean lines and key information prominent on the page:

On the same note your copy (i.e.: what's written on your website) needs to be engaging. You want to tell people about who you are, invite them to come to your establishment, make them want to come and eat with you.

Here's an example of great copy for the Waterside Inn in Bray, UK. When you read it see how it sets the scene for what to expect, as well as answering questions people may have (will it be overly formal as it's such a great restaurant):

"An enchanting riverside setting... elegant surroundings, with a relaxed, unpretentious atmosphere... effortless, yet impeccable, service... and of course, exquisite cuisine, as befits a three-star Michelin establishment... Welcome to the Waterside Inn... and to a world-class culinary experience.

Nestling on the banks of the Thames, in the charming 16th century village of Bray, this delightful 'restaurant with rooms' has been serving inspirational French cuisine since 1972. Its welcoming, informal ambience belies its formidable reputation: owned by the celebrated Roux père et fils, and nowadays run by Alain Roux, the Waterside is renowned across the globe as a leading light in the world of gastronomy."

Another vital aspect of your website, is ensuring that it is mobile phone-friendly. The majority of people now search for restaurant using mobile phones.

According to a Nielsen Survey[1] 95% of smart phone users regularly search for restaurants on their phones, with a staggering 90% of those actually going into a restaurant

---

[1] Figures from a report commissioned by Nielson: http://www.nielsen.com

within 24 hours. **64% go in within 1 hour**.

77% of the USA adult population now own a smart phone[2], with 80% in the UK[3].

If your website isn't mobile-enabled and somebody visits it using their phone, in all likelihood your website will be unreadable or unusable to them, so you'll lose them as a potential customer.

There are 2 types of "sins" you find with websites that aren't mobile enabled.

1. They shrink everything so it is unreadable

---

[2] http://www.pewinternet.org/fact-sheet/mobile/
[3] http://www.bbc.co.uk/news/business-37468560

2. They don't shrink and your site is massive on their phone

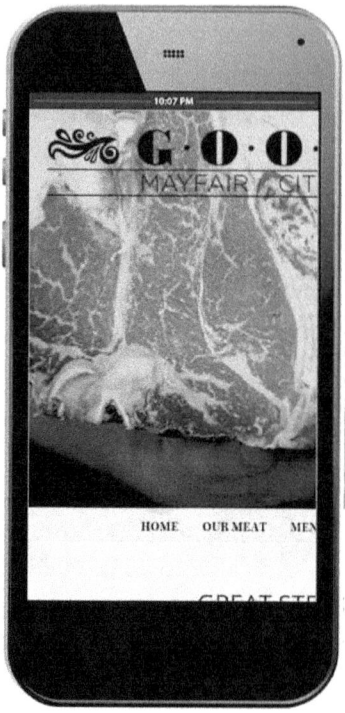

Either of these issues will mean that rather than considering you as somewhere to go and eat, they will take the easy option, hit the "back" button and find a restaurant whose information they can actually access.

You've got a very short time to grab their attention, and if your site isn't working on their phone you'll be missing out on a huge tranche of the market that might come and eat with you.

Key Points:

YOUR WEBSITE MUST

* Look modern and professional
* Have engaging copy
* Be mobile-friendly

The 4 Key Website Elements

There are four key elements which your website needs to focus on, and these are things that people generally get wrong in our community.

1 – Your Menu

Firstly, the menu. If you look at the majority of restaurant websites, the menu is a PDF document. Now the bad news is that PDFs, while they do work on mobile phones now, still have to be downloaded.

They take *time* to be downloaded.

Your user - your potential customer - has to click a button, download the PDF, then open it up in order to see what they might be able to eat at your restaurant.

This is a massive pain in the backside, and they're likely to just lose interest and move on to greener pastures.

Never underestimate how short an attention span you're working with online (we're all the same – how many hoops will you jump through online for a business you don't know from Adam, before getting irritated and moving on?). So, at all costs, avoid having PDFs for your menus.

2 – Contact Us

The second element is having a really good Contact Us page and details. On your Contact Us page you need to include a few things: a contact form in case a customer wants to contact you but doesn't want to call you, plus a map so they can visualise where you are. You also need to have your full contact details (phone, address and email) on this page, which brings us onto our 3rd element

3 – Contact Details on Every Page

You need to have your contact details on *every single page of the website.* Ideally you want to have your contact details "above the fold".

Above the fold is a marketing phrase which means the area of a website page which is visible without having to scroll down.

You want your contact details immediately visible when someone visits your website, no matter which page they arrive at, so they'll automatically be able to see where you are.

The header of your website is an ideal place to put your contact details – the header looks the same on every page of a website, and is right at the top (the logo often goes here too).

4 – Online Booking / Reservation

The final element is that it's really important to have some sort of online booking.

This shouldn't be just a contact us form which potential customers fill out and then you call them back. That's not ideal: people want an immediate result.

If you can't afford to have a bespoke online booking system built - which a lot of people in our community can't - then there loads of websites out there that can help you out (most of them are really simple to integrate with your existing website).

Go to www.google.com and type in the search term "free online reservation system for restaurants" to find a selection of possible people to work with.

Some may charge a small fee but it's well worth it and you'll see a positive uplift in people booking to come and eat at your restaurant.

Key Points:

WEBSITE ESSENTIALS

* Menus (not PDFs)

* Contact Us page with contact form & map

* Contact details above the fold on every webpage

* Provide online booking

ONLINE BUSINESS PAGES: How do I set up my Online Business Pages to get customers?

The Online Business Pages are one of the most overlooked part of restaurant business strategy. If you go to Google and type in, for example, "French restaurant in London", at the top of the page the first three results are coming directly from Google's Online Business Pages.

It's a little piece of valuable online real estate which Google gives you, where you can enter your information and entice customers to come to your restaurant before they go to your website. It's called **Google My Business**.

Your Online Business Page is very easy to set up, you just need to go to https://www.google.com/business/ and follow the setup process.

The first thing they will ask you to do is "Verify" your business. This is to make sure that you are the real owner, and not someone else trying to claim the listing.

Google will typically send you a little card in the post which will have a verification code on it. This can take one to two weeks to arrive but once it does follow their instructions to pop in the verification code, and then you're able to complete your profile.

Once you've done that, take every opportunity to fill in your details:

- ➢ add an introduction to say who you are
- ➢ your business hours opening hours
- ➢ the type of food you serve
- ➢ any special offers you might have on any particular days of the week

Ensure that you also include lots of photos of your establishment – preferably including some of you and some of your staff – and also some of the food.

Finally, if you possibly can, include some short videos too.

That's it! You've now completed you Google My Business page.

Let's take a look at your Social Media profiles now.

KEY POINTS:

GOOGLE BUSINESS PAGE

* Include introduction & hours
* Include all business details
* Add any Special Offers
* Add photos & video (if possible)

SOCIAL MEDIA: Can social media really help with increasing my covers?

The answer is "Yes" – social media is vital.

It has changed quite a lot in the last few years – if you'd asked me that question four years ago my answer would not have been as emphatic. But with the way that Facebook especially has shaped up, changing the way that it does business and engages with its users, it's now becoming more and more critical.

There are five main platforms that you want to look at as a restaurant owner, and in order of importance they are:

- ➢ Facebook
- ➢ Instagram
- ➢ YouTube
- ➢ Twitter
- ➢ Pinterest.

Now, that's quite a few and there's quite a lot that can be done with each one, but for the sake of giving you the most effective thing that you can do immediately, you want to concentrate on Facebook: it will give you the most results for the effort put in..

The first thing you need to do on Facebook is set up your business page. If you have one already that's great, but if not then go to Facebook and log in to your personal account (to be an "Admin" of a Facebook business page you need to have a personal Facebook account first). From here you will have the option to "create a page", where you'll choose the category as being a business type, and then you want to add your full business details.

Alternatively you can start here: https://en-gb.facebook.com/business/learn/set-up-facebook-page

Step 1 – Create your Page

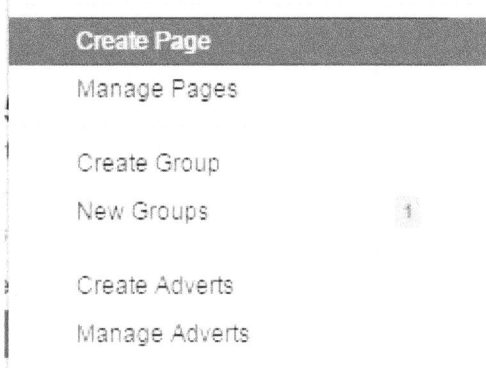

Step 2 – Choose your Business Type (go for "Local Business or Place")

Step 3 – Enter your Basic Business Details

Local business or place

Select a category

Business or place name

Street address

City/County

Postcode

Phone

By clicking Get Started, you agree to the Facebook Pages Terms.

Get Started

Once you've created your Facebook business page, you then want to create an "About" sub-page. There are several sub-pages available within a Facebook business page and arguably the most important is the About page, because people will visit it and expect to find out who you are, when you're open and what kind of food you're serving.

It's also important to add your menus - something which 99% of restaurants don't do on their Facebook pages. A photo is fine as this is something that people expect to see on Facebook (you'd NEVER want a photo for your menu on your actual website!).

Remember that Facebook could be the first touchpoint (point at which someone actually engages with you as a business) that somebody might have with you – maybe they've seen one of their friends has liked you, or your Facebook page came up on Google, or you're doing some kind of marketing to drive them to the page – so you want to make sure that they can see as much as they can about your restaurant without having to leave Facebook, without having to go to your website.

Step 4 – Edit your "About Us Page"

Choose...

About

Then...

Edit Page Info

Then fill in as much info as possible!

Now that you have an "About" sub-page, the next step is to add a cover photo and then create some posts.

I'd recommend that you create three posts. The first post will be a "Welcome to our page" post: an introduction to who you are, simply saying something along the lines of "Hello and welcome, we hope you enjoy visiting our page and if you have any questions please just get in touch with us".

You are then going to make this post what they call "sticky" i.e.: it will always stick to the top of the page (we'll show you how in a minute!)

The next post you create will contain some recent news - something that is topical and might be of interest to your potential customers. Perhaps you've created a new menu item, something seasonal, or you've been involved with something interesting in the local community? These are the kinds of news items to include.

Your third post is going to be a recipe for people to try at home: give them an indication of the kind of food you're serving by giving them one of you recipes to try. Don't worry about whether or not it's something everyone will be able to cook.

If the recipe is a bit beyond their cooking skills, that's not necessarily a bad thing because it demonstrates the kind of skill which is going into your dishes. However, if it's a recipe they can cook and they try it and it's delicious (which I'm sure it will be) then they'll think "Wow, if this is what they give us to try at home then imagine what their food must be like in the restaurant!"

Step 6 – Add a Cover Photo

Click...

Then...

You can then either "Upload" an image (preferable of your restaurant) or choose from an existing photo you've already uploaded.

Step 7 – Add a Post and Make it Sticky

First choose...

Write a Note

Then write something, add a photo and publish. Once publish click on the post options and choose...

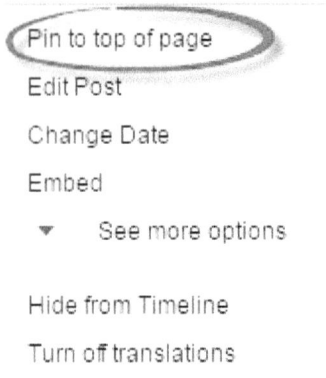

Once you have successfully created your first three posts, you need to ask everyone you know to "Like" your page. This is especially important if you've got a new page which doesn't have many people liking it.

There's a marketing/psychological term called "Social Proof" which describes the fact that people respond to seeing other people believing in a product or a brand (or a restaurant, in this case). By having people like your page, other people will come and think, for example "If these 200 people like the page, the restaurant must be good, so maybe I'll like it and maybe I'll go and try them".

The more people who like your page, the more social proof this creates and the more validity it lends to your restaurant.

Now, you may be thinking that getting likes from people other than your friends is going to be pretty challenging, but actually it's very easy.

To prove this I set up a Facebook restaurant page about six months ago – I got a few initial likes to it and have literally done nothing to it since. This restaurant doesn't even *exist*, it's just a figment of my imagination, but I set it up using the same methods I've just described, and as of today it has 1,123 likes. Every week the page is getting another 30 or 40 people who actively like this imaginary restaurant, so I highly recommend you take this step for your own restaurant.

Imagine how many likes you could be getting for your restaurant, which actually exists! Don't be afraid, it will happen, just follow the instructions I've given you here and be proactive in putting useful information on your page.

KEY POINTS:

FACEBOOK BUSINESS PAGE

* Create "About" sub-page
* Three posts – Welcome, News & Recipe
* Make Welcome post sticky
* Ask people you know for likes

ONLINE REVIEW SITES: How important are review sites, and how can I get reviews (even negative ones) to work for me?

Review sites are essential to restaurant marketing.

In the previous section we talked about Social Proof, and how a person's attitude to something can be influenced by seeing the opinions of others. Review websites like TripAdvisor or Google reviews are the epitome of this.

As you're probably aware, on these websites customers can go and write a review after they've been to your restaurant, give you a score out of 5 stars, and will typically make comments as well - either positive or negative. You then end up with a weighted score which affects your standing and positon within the site.

For example with TripAdvisor (which is the Big Daddy of all the review sites) you are ranked based on:

> ➤ how *many* reviews you have
> ➤ how *frequently* you are being reviewed
> ➤ and the *quality* of those reviews i.e.: your star-level score on those reviews.

Ranking well on TripAdvisor can automatically bring you in new customers.

The second most important review website to focus on is Google reviews – these reviews show up on your Google Business Page.

The typical lifecycle of somebody searching online for a new restaurant is: go to a search engine (eg: Google) and type in the restaurant type and the town, for example "Italian food Bournemouth".

The next thing they're most likely to do is click on one of the top three Business Page listings, if available, or they'll look for a TripAdvisor result such as "The 10 Best Italian Restaurants in Bournemouth". Once they click on the TripAdvisor or Google link, they'll scan through the results and see what the reviews are like for those restaurants.

Unfortunately, something that can happen and does happen is that people will post negative reviews.

Negative reviews may come whether you provide excellent service or not – they are a fact of life and they may be justified or unjustified (you may have had an off day, or the customer may have had an off day and felt the urge to post a negative review for their own reasons). Regardless, the key thing to do is respond to all reviews, even the negative ones - and I would say *especially* the negative ones.

With negative reviews, take responsibility wherever possible for the customer's dissatisfaction, regardless of the tone of their review.

If you can honestly not see a single way you could have done better on the occasion in question, then still respond positively in a non-offensive and non-aggressive way, for example:

"Dear XX, Thank you for taking the time to give us your feedback. We totally understand your position and although we feel we did our very best for you, we are sorry to hear that you didn't enjoy yourself with us".

The key thing is to be nice about it, no matter what they say: bear in mind that in addition to talking to that one person, perhaps more importantly **you are also being heard by roomfuls of potential customers**. It's not in your interest to drive those people away for the sake of one unhappy customer.

Another important note on responding to reviews:

Personalise each response.

If you post virtually the same response to every review, you are missing out on the opportunity to come across as a business which genuinely cares about each customer.

Here are a few examples from TripAdvisor of good ways to respond to both positive and negative reviews:

Great response with personalisation to a positive review[4]

"What a gem!"

⊛⊛⊛⊛⊛ Reviewed 14 October 2016

Amazing coffee and the best club sandwich I have ever tried. The whole ethos of the place is impressive. the service is excellent and they use all natural high quality ingredients. What more could you ask for?

Helpful?　👍 Thank martinethicalint2016　🚩 Report

Garphie T, Owner at Guavavibe, responded to this review

Thank you so much for your review! We're so happy you've enjoyed your experience and your club sandwich. We're going to work hard for your next visit to find that one more thing you didn't even know you could ask for!

More ▼

---

[4] https://www.tripadvisor.co.uk/Restaurant_Review-g186262-d9600726-Reviews-Guavavibe-Bournemouth_Dorset_England.html

Here's an example of a good response to a complaint:

"Below average "

⊛⊛◯◯◯ Reviewed 23 October 2016   ▢ via mobile

Quite many recommended this Italian in Altrincham and I must say I was disappointed. Staff quite arrogant and when we told the other dish pasta is raw we were told pasta must be al dente. Well there is difference having al dente to not enough cooked pasta. They made the dish again and no difference. I can just say over prised food and service could be friendlier.

Visited October 2016

Less ▲

Helpful?   👍   2   Thank minlisvir   ⚐ Report

See all 3 reviews by minlisvir for Altrincham
Ask minlisvir about Sugo Pasta Kitchen

Sugo P, Owner at Sugo Pasta Kitchen, responded to this review. 25 October 2016

Dear reviewer

I decided to respond to your review as it was myself who came from the kitchen to speak to you last Saturday, and I feel that your version of events is slightly unfair. Also, because the cooking of pasta is understandably a matter very close to our hearts!

I was made aware that you felt your pasta was too hard, and after trying the dish my honest appraisal was that it wasn't. I came from the kitchen to explain how and why we cook pasta the way we do but also said that I was really happy to make the dish again as I wanted you to enjoy your meal, to which you declined. A few minutes later your waitress brought the dish back as you wanted it remade. To remake the dish at this point would of taken 20 mins so we did our best to cook the pasta more in the pan (trying not to overcook the other elements). You also had diverged from the menu, something we advise against doing as each element has its rightful place!

Just so you are aware, the majority of pasta in Italian restaurants in England is so soft because it is pre-cooked (something that we vehemently oppose) and not of great quality, which means that it loses its structure. Southern Italians eat pasta al dente, often more so than you experienced and we have stuck to our principles on this since we opened (to the delight of most of our customers) Can I suggest (and sorry to sound arrogant, but this is my professional opinion) that you have been conditioned (by brit-italian restaurants) to think that pasta should be soft?

If it is the pre cooked, anglo italian version of pasta you prefer to eat in restaurants im sorry to say that Sugo Pasta Kitchen probably isn't for you. If on the other hand you'd be willing to let us show you that there is another way (no deviating from the menu, taking each dish as it comes) we'd be delighted to see you again

Have a great week
Alex (co-owner)

Report response as inappropriate

Finally... I just want to re-iterate the need to respond to ALL reviews. Tripadvisor have published stats showing that the average review goes up with the amount of responses seen:

Rate of Management Response for Recent Reviews vs. Average Review Rating

0% response rate = 3.81 average review rating
5% – 40% response rate = 4.04 average review rating
40% – 65% = 4.05 average review rating
65%+ response rate = 4.15 average review rating

Please respond to all reviews!

On the subject of TripAdvisor I want to mention a technique which I recommend, which isn't cost-free, but it only costs you once you have acquired a booking. That technique is offering online booking through TripAdvisor.

You may have noticed that when you go and look at a listing for a restaurant or a hotel on TripAdvisor, it often gives you the ability to book online. This can be a great way to get new customers to book directly from TripAdvisor, which a lot of potential customers will be attracted to due to the convenience. Most people want the easiest, quickest route to getting that they want – the easiest customer journey.

For restaurant bookings, TripAdvisor works in conjunction with the website The Fork (https://www.theforkmanager.com).

You will pay 4 euros per booking (£3.40 or 4.30 US dollars as I write this) – half of which goes to TripAdvisor and the other half to The Fork. They also have some paid monthly subscription options, but these won't be necessary if you follow the steps outlined later in this book when we start to talk about getting customers coming back for more.[5]

Consider what it would normally cost you to acquire a new customer, and it may well be that 4 euros is a reasonable amount for a booking you may not otherwise have got.

If you're questioning whether that customer would have just booked via your own website if TripAdvisor booking wasn't available, I would say that if a customer is likely to move to your website, they will do that anyway i.e.: they'll hop off TripAdvisor and onto your website as a next step (where of course you will have ensured that a very easy route to book is available).

But if they're not the sort of person to research across a lot of websites and just wants a quick booking without leaving TripAdvisor, you don't want to lose them at that point, you want to grab them and get that booking.

So in summary, by offering TripAdvisor booking in addition to online booking on your own website, you have covered all bases: customers who want to learn more before booing, and also customers who want a quick solution now.

REVIEW WEBSITES

* Focus on Tripadvisor & Google reviews

* Respond positively to every review

* Individualise each review (don't cut-and-paste)

* Offer booking directly from Tripadvisor

---

[5] https://www.theforkmanager.com/prices/

PAGE INTENTIONALLY LEFT BLANK

CHAPTER THREE

Paid Online Advertising

How do I use the internet to advertise my restaurant?

There are three main places where I recommend you should be advertising, in order to get new customers into your restaurant.

> ➤ The first is on Google, using something called Pay Per Click (PPC).

> ➤ The second is using Facebook to create an advertising campaign.

> ➤ Finally I recommend using YouTube to attract new customers.

How much should I be spending on Advertising?

This is the question I'm most often asked, and it comes down to being able to answer one question.

What is a typical Customer Lifetime Value to your restaurant?

> "In marketing, customer lifetime value (CLV) (or often CLTV), lifetime customer value (LCV), or life-time value (LTV) is a prediction of the net profit attributed to the entire future relationship with a customer."

In a nutshell it's how much a customer is going to be worth to us over our entire relationship with them.

Let's dig a bit deeper into this so you are totally clear, as this number is going to be really important to your future success.

What we're trying to work out here is how much (in $ or £) profit a customer is likely to bring into your restaurant over the entire time they are a customer (so including repeat visits).

So, of example, if your typical customer spends $25 (as an individual, not a whole group), and your average booking size is 3.5 people, then you know that a typical customer coming to your restaurant is worth $25 x 3.5, so $87.50 gross.

Now let's say they come to you 3 times a year, and keep coming back for the next 4 years. You can now work out their total lifetime gross value as:

$87.50 x 3 x 4 = $1,050

We now need to plug in you profit margin. For this example we'll use 25% as clear profit after costs.

Your total lifetime customer value is then 25% x $1,050 which is $262.50.

What this tells us is we shouldn't be afraid to spend a bit of money to get new customers in.

BUT... HOLD ON... I'm not telling you to spend $262.50 for each customer... that would be crazy!

However if we know we're going to earn this much clear profit from a customer over their lifetime with us, wouldn't it be a good idea to be prepared to spend money to get them in?

As a rule of thumb this is how I work out how much to spend on getting a new customer through my door. Time for a little bit more maths... sorry!

Let's revisit the gross profit on the first visit - $87.50. Let's work out you net profit (25% of this amount, which is $21.87).

Divide this figure in half, and you've got yourself a reasonable figure to spend for each customer you want to get in (let's round this to $10 to make life easy!).

So... if you want to get 2 new customers (bookings with 3.5 people so 7 covers in total) a day, then you should be happy to spend $20 a day on your marketing to new customers.

Now the reality is that it probably won't actually cost you that much as very few restaurants are using online paid media to attract new customers, so you won't be facing much competition (which means you pay less for each potential visitor).

This was a pretty complicated section, and if you'd like to read some more information on how to calculate the Customer Lifetime Value, here are a couple of good ones:

https://blog.kissmetrics.com/how-to-calculate-lifetime-value/

https://upserve.com/blog/restaurant-guest-lifetime-value/

Let's move on to getting you some customers!

What is Pay Per Click (PPC) and how do I use it?

Often, when you search for something on Google – for example "private dining London" – you'll see one or more listings which appear right at the top of the page, even above the Google Business Page listings. These results at the very top of the page are paid advertising – Pay Per Click (PPC) ads. They allow you to appear at the top of the search engine rankings, right in front of a customer searching specifically for what you offer.

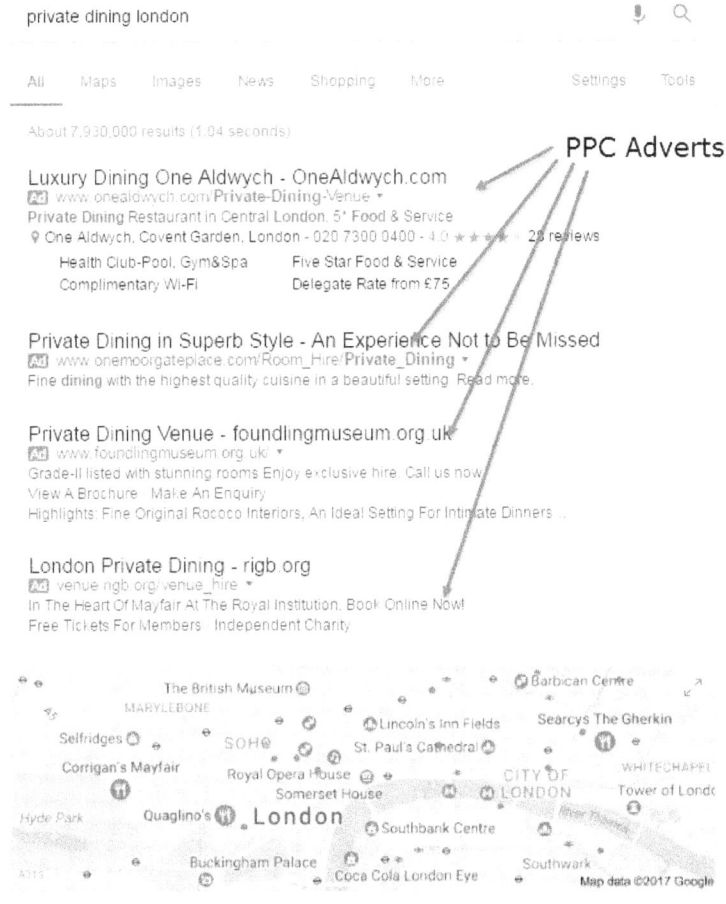

The first big advantage of this is that you can immediately get to the top of the Google results page: you don't have to employ anyone to do your Search Engine Optimisation, or to do any work to get you up the rankings. You can be incredibly and highly targeted with it.

The second big advantage is that **you only pay when somebody actually clicks on your advert**.

In some advertising forms, you pay whenever your advert *appears* on a website, even if the potential customer doesn't even see it, click on it, or show any interest in it. This is known as Pay Per View or Cost Per View. We want to avoid that kind of advertising at all costs - we only really want to pay when people are actually taking action (by going to your restaurant website).

If you are that restaurant with a private dining room in London, and someone sees your advert at the top of the page, they're going to click on it if it's a good compelling advert.

So what makes a "good, compelling advert"?

Firstly, it has a great headline - something that attracts the customer initially. Then comes a good body, which makes an offer of some sort, a reason for them to come and visit your restaurant or website with a "call to action". Finally, make use of ad extensions – opportunities which Google gives you, to input further business details.

If you go now and type into Google "private dining London" you'll see an advert appear. The heading is in blue, the body is in grey, and below that there are further links in blue. Those links are the ad extension opportunities, and for a lot of business they say things like "Contact Us", "About Us", "Services We Offer" etc. For your restaurant, the ad extensions I recommend including are Contact us, Special Deals and Menu. The menu is the number one thing people always want to look at, so if they can just click and go straight to your menu that's great - it makes it much more likely that people are going to click on your advert.

Luxury Dining One Aldwych - Covent Garden - onealdwych.com
Ad www.onealdwych.com/Private-Dining ▼
Private Dining Restaurant in Central London. 5* Food & Service
5* Central London Hotel · Best Price Guarantee · Free WiFi · No Booking Fees
Health Club-Pool, Gym&Spa · Martini Movies - £42.50 · Complimentary Wi-Fi

The above advert was first in for the private dining search at the time of publishing this book. You can see they have a clear headline **Luxury Dining One Aldwych** and the body goes on to mention some features (Private Dining, 5* Food, Free Wi-Fi, No Booking Fees).

So... apart from an OK headline, a pretty terrible advert. There is no "reason why" you should choose them. No booking and free wi-fi imply that this is a generic advert for hotel clients that they are showing it to people looking for private dining.

BIG MISTAKE... You need to make sure you advert speaks to the people who you want to attract, and this advert will put off people looking for private dining.

On a more positive note, they have included extensions, although they are totally irrelevant to this search term.

It's worth knowing that if you provide ad extensions and create a good advert, Google will charge you less for your click than, say, the other restaurant which didn't include the ad extensions and didn't set up the ad in the way I've mentioned (which is Google's recommended best practice).

Your rival could be paying 1 or 2 dollars for a click and you could be paying 50 cents.

Another way to create a more effective Google PPC ad is to target by location and demographics.

Locations ? Which locations do you want to target (or exclude) in your campaign?

       All countries and territories

  ● United Kingdom

       Let me choose...

Enter a location to target or exclude   Advanced search

For example, a country, city, region or postcode

When you're setting up your PPC account, you can choose to advertise only within a set radius of your business location. Certainly for restaurants, I recommend that you never advertise for a distance further than 8km (5 miles) from your restaurant – you want to target people who are either within walking distance, or a very easy drive to your restaurant.

Unless you're absolutely out in the middle of nowhere and there's no customer base within 5 miles of you, then the best use of your money is to target people who are most likely to actually want to come to your restaurant.

You don't want to be paying for clicks by people who live at the other end of the country and have no chance whatsoever of coming to see you. Here's how you do it:

STEP 1
Choose "Advanced Search"

Advanced search

STEP 2

Choose "Radius Targeting"

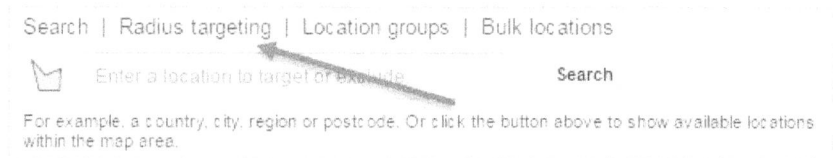

STEP 3

Enter your postcode, set radius to 5 miles and click Search

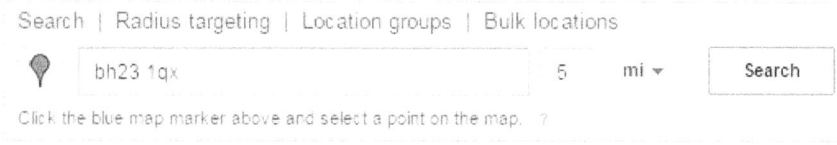

STEP 4

You'll now be show a radius from your location. Click "Add" and then "Done"

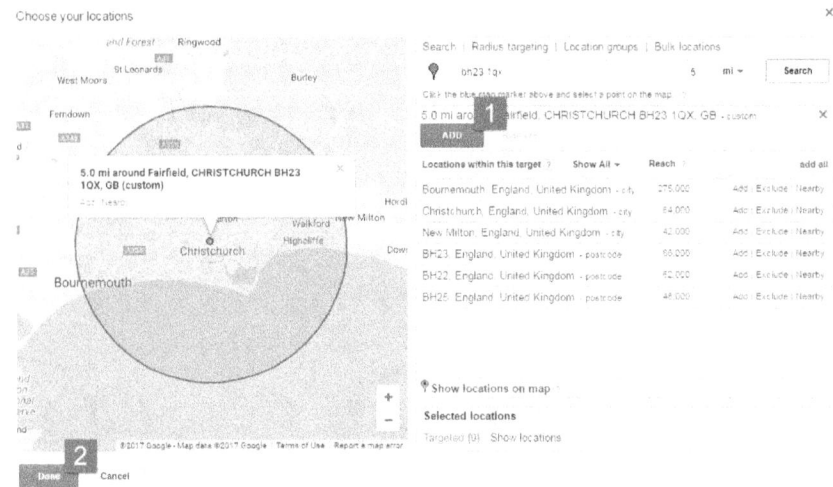

Google will now display you targeting options...

Google offers the additional option to target by time of day - you can opt to pay slightly more at certain times of day to make your ad likely to be served above a competitor ad. The benefit of this is that, if you know that the prime time somebody is likely to be searching for a Greek restaurant in San Francisco is between the hours of 11.30am and 1pm, you can pay a little more to be ranked higher during this time. This puts you on the customer's radar in the lunch service time. The same principle applies if you know that people are potentially searching between 5 and 6pm after work.

The last thing you need to think about is what are called "Keywords". A keyword is the word someone types into Google when they're looking for somewhere to eat. Your job is to choose the right keywords for your PPC account so when someone searches for a particular kind of restaurant, your advert appears.

You want to be as specific as possible when choosing them. Most restaurants will go for something like

Restaurant + Town

So "Restaurant in New York" or "Restaurant London".

This is a mistake.

You want to be more specific and include the type of cuisine you serve. If you are an Italian restaurant, you would have a keyword like "Italian Restaurant in New York".

This way, people who want Italian food would find you, and be more likely to click on you advert. In the former example, someone searching for a generic restaurant in New York might hate Italian, so you are wasting your time showing them your advert. Even worse, they might be undecided, click on your advert (which costs you) and then decide they fancy Chinese instead!

Pay Per Click advertising is also available on Bing, which is Microsoft's search network. It follows exactly the same rules, guidelines and schedules.

I would always recommend that you use Google first because that's where 80% of the search engine traffic is going to be. However, when you do decide to add Bing into your advertising mix, when you come to set up your Bing account you'll find that they offer a very simple procedure whereby you can import all your Google settings. This means that within a few minutes you'll have your Bing account and advertising campaign set up. Initially, though, just focus on getting the Google PPC working for you, then expand to using Bing as well.

PAY PER CLICK (PPC)

* Attract people with your headline
* Put an offer or reason to visit in the body of the ad
* Use ad extensions
* Target location (also demographics & time of day)
* Use Google first, then add Bing

How do I create a Facebook advertising campaign?

The first thing you need to do to create a Facebook advertising campaign, is to set up your Facebook business page which we covered in the previous chapter. Once you've got your Facebook page running, the next step is to create something called a "promoted post". In order to do this you need to create a post on your page, in which you'll make an offer to your customers.

Facebook are always changing the way you can do this, and currently they are trialing "New Post Options".

Within this new set-up, you want to choose "Create an offer". As of time of writing this is a brand new post option which means people can:

> ➤ Save the offer
> ➤ Get notified about it (to remind them to take the offer

This should help our potential customers actually take the offer up.

Create an Offer

However, this ONLY applies if you are offering:

> ➤ A % discount
> ➤ An money discount
> ➤ Buy one, get one free
> ➤ Free stuff (i.e. free desert with every main purchased)

If you want offer something else (e.g. fixed price meal for 2 with a glass of wine) then choose "Get Bookings" if you have online booking enabled, or the "Write a Note" option. For these 2 options, the overall strategy for writing your advert and then boosting your post does not change.

Let's carry on talking about "Create an Offer"

STEP 1 – Choose Availability

This lets people know where they can redeem the offer. We want to set this to "in store"

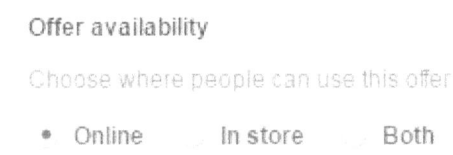

STEP 2 – Choose the "Offer Type"

Choose this depending on your offer. In this example we're doing a % discount

STEP 3 – Add your post content

Firstly, create a headline, something along the lines of "November Special Offer", "January Deal" or "Valentine's day Special" – obviously this can apply to any month, week or day if you want to. You're aiming to deliver an eye catching headline which will make customers want to read more.

After the headline, you want to make an offer within the description field. The offer will be something along the lines of "10% off your meal throughout November", or it may be "Free soft drink with every main course ordered in November".

You now want to add a photo that illustrates your offer. Ideally use a shot from your restaurant, but if you're struggling for a creative you always visit one of the many free photo sites which will provide you images for free:

https://pixabay.com/
https://www.pexels.com/
http://www.stockvault.net/

If you're doing another type of post (e.g. "Get Bookings"), you then want to have a deadline, such as "Offer ends 30th November".

For the "Create an Offer" post, you set the expiry date for your offer and Facebook automatically populates this for you.

STEP 4 – Add an Expiry Date

Choose the date your offer ends

Expiry date

23/2/2017

Next, you need to include a code for them to give you, which is unique to this particular advert.

Again, this post type gives you the option to do this as a set field, but if you're using one of the other post types you'll finish off your post with something like "Simply quote discount code NOV17 on arrival".

Step 5 – Add an Offer Code

Code type

Choose how this offer will be used at checkout

• Discount code   Barcode   No code

11/20

FBMARCH2017

The reason you need to have a code is that you'll want to be able to know that this person has come from seeing your Facebook ad (and which Facebook ad, if you have more than one on the go). Then you'll be able to easily track how many people have been to your restaurant based on this advert.

You'll also be able to measure whether one of your ads is proving more effective than another.

The last thing you need to with this post is add any terms and conditions. In this section you might want to add "excludes drinks" if you are offering money off the food bill only, but feel free to pop in whatever exclusions are important to you.

Step 6 – Add Terms and Conditions

Terms and conditions (optional) 🛈   0/5000

This space is for the important rules and legal details about you

You'll see that as you are creating you Offer post, Facebook show you how this is going to look to potential customers.

IMPORTANT – most people are going to be seeing this on their mobile phones, so make sure to click on "Mobile News Feed" to ensure your post looks great on mobile phones

Here's what a sample post might look like:

Once you've created the post as described, click "boost post".

STEP 7 – Boost Your Post

Boost Post

We now move on to the process of customer targeting.

Customer targeting on Facebook involves the same principles we discussed earlier regarding Google PPC. You'll be targeting people within a specific distance from your restaurant, and again (unless you're out in the middle of nowhere) it's best to stick to a maximum distance of 8km from the restaurant.

Having clicked "boost post", choose "Create New Audience" then give your audience a Name (e.g. "Target Customers")

Ignore Gender for now and move onto location.

If this has already been populated for you, then remove by clicking the x on the right hand side of the location, then type in your postcode/zipcode and Facebook will then present a map with your location pinned against that area code, but it only applies to that code, and is not much use to us...

STEP 8 – Type in your Business Postcode

The good news is there is an option to add a pin on the map, so grab that pin and drop it as near to the existing pin that's currently on the map as possible. Facebook will then give you the ability to specify a radius of 5m.

STEP 9 – Drop a Pin

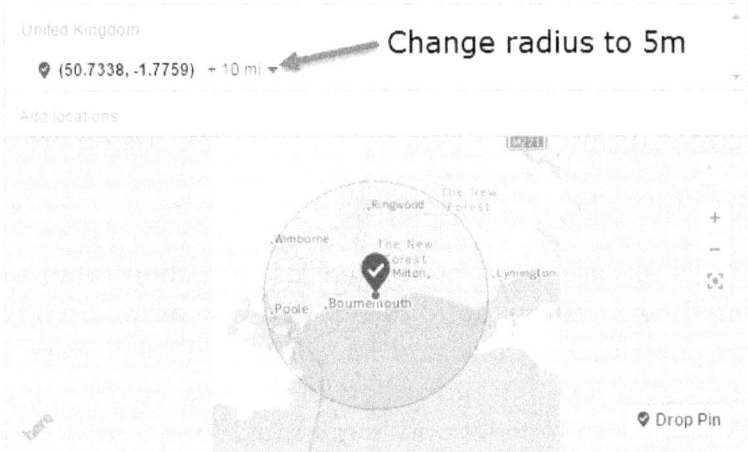

After this, you want to pick your customers based on their age, gender and likes.

So if you're a restaurant that wants to attract a younger crowd and you only want people aged between 18 and 30 coming to your restaurant, you can select the option of people aged between 18 and 30.

The post will then only be served to people within that age range within an 8km radius from your restaurant. If you're a vegetarian restaurant, you can choose people who are vegetarian as your targeting, or if you want people who like Indian food, you can choose Indian food. So you can be very specific, and I would say at this point, the more specific the better, especially if you really know who you are or if you have a restaurant which is very niche.

STEP 10 – Choose Customer Interests, Age and Gender

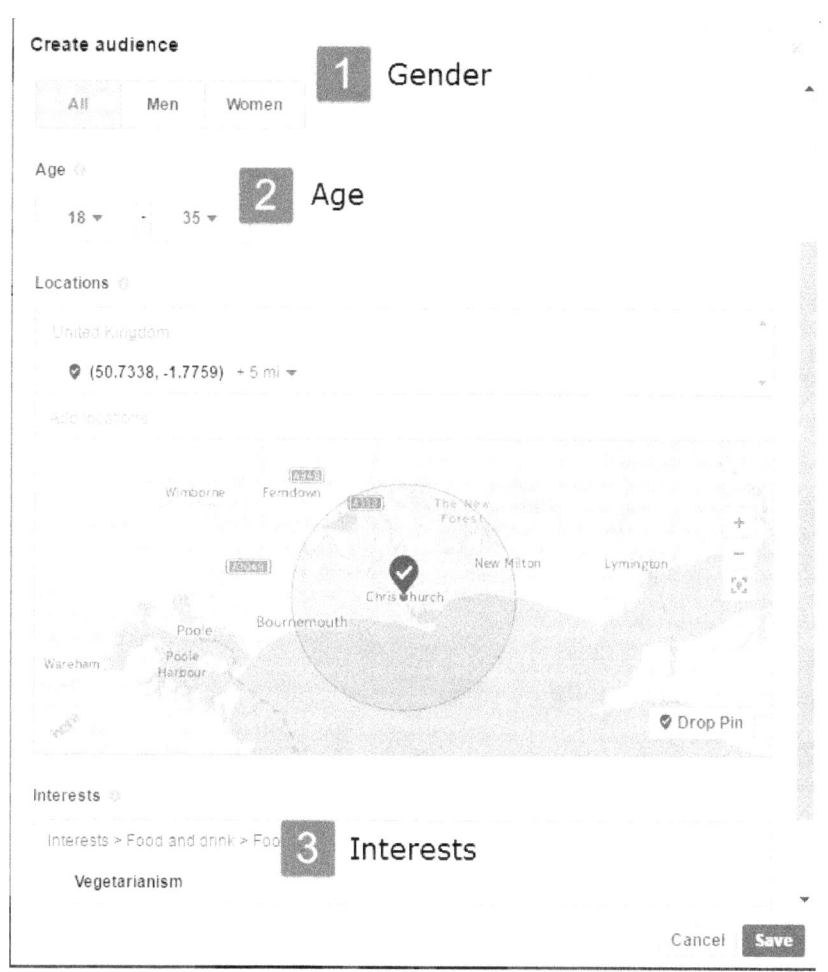

Save this audience, then set your budget – I recommend putting in £10 a day (or $15 a day) – again this depends on how much you are able to spend on getting new customers in, but this will be fine for testing your offer. As with PPC, you are only charged when people actually interact with your post. Some people will click on "Get Offer" and others will scribble down the promotion and come and see you.

It's a great way of getting in front of the right kinds of people within a reasonable radius of your restaurant, and you've got a special offer there so you can actually track the ad's success and see what your return on investment is.

FACEBOOK ADVERTISING

* Use a compelling headline, offer & a deadline

* Include a Special Offer Code

* Target your ad

* Track the outcome by using the code

How can I use YouTube to get new customers?

YouTube is probably the most under-utilised medium in the restaurant community. Restaurateurs do use Pay Per Click and Facebook, but both of them are used sparingly (and I'm sorry to say, often incorrectly). The best use of YouTube in this case is something called "retargeting".

Have you ever been to a website to look at a product - for example to Amazon to look at a coffee maker - and then you've gone to another website and seen an advert for that same coffee maker appear randomly, even though you're not on Amazon anymore? Then you go to another website, and that same advert will appear on that website too? The coffee maker is following you all over the internet. That's "retargeting".

A website can have something called a pixel placed on it, which is basically a little line of code that tracks the visitor from the page they were looking at, all around the internet. Wherever the customer goes, ads are going to try and attract them back to buy that coffee maker.

You can use this idea effectively for your restaurant via YouTube. If you've ever watched a YouTube video you'll have seen that adverts pop up when you're first about to watch the video. You can get your advert to appear at the beginning of YouTube videos, but only to people who have already been to your restaurant website – this gets them back to thinking about a visit to your restaurant.

Ideally your YouTube advert should be a video set in your restaurant. This can be as simple as somebody cooking, or some ambient shots within your restaurant.

When a visitor comes to your restaurant website, you can then set your advert to appear when they are next watching a video on YouTube using retargeting.

However you still need to follow our guidelines on creating an advert:

- ➢ A Clear Headline
- ➢ A Clear Offer (reason why they should come)
- ➢ A Clear Call to Action
- ➢ A Deadline
- ➢ A Voucher Code (to help you track the ads success).

You can add all of the above in text over your video or using spoken word (although definitely best to have the Voucher Code as text also so there's no confusion).

If you're unable to get a video done, you can create a very effective photo / video animation at a website called Animoto (https://animoto.com/)

Here you can upload photos and / or videos and Animoto will animated them for you to help create a compelling advert.

There is a costs associated to this, though (£39.99 a month at time of publishing), but you can always sign up for 1 month, create a bunch of videos and then cancel your membership... It's totally up to you.

These guys are great, though, so please check out the site and some of their sample videos.

If you don't have any photos or video there is one last option you can explore called VideoScribe (http://www.videoscribe.co)

These guys let you do what's known as a sketch video. You may have seen them before – a hand appears in the video and draws out the sales message. They're still very effective, so if you have no other option, use these guys. The cost per month is £18 at time of publishing.

For more information on retargeting and Youtube, visit our

blog http://www.therestaurantmarketer.com/blog

In summary, Google PPC, Facebook advertising and YouTube retargeting are the three key methods I recommend that you action. From an online paid advertising point of view, these are currently the fastest, most effective and cost effective ways of bringing new customers into your restaurant.

YOUTUBE ADVERTISING

* Show Adverts to People Who Visited Your Website
* Either make a Video, use Animoto or Videoscribe
* Make sure you follow our guidelines on creating
an effective advert

Although we have talked about free online ways of attracting customers, those methods do still take time (and your time is money!). So as long as you can achieve a good return on investment for spending money on paid advertising, then it's definitely worth doing.

PAGE INTENTIONALLY LEFT BLANK

CHAPTER FOUR

Offline Marketing

How can I attract new customers using offline methods?

There are three main ways that you can use to get new customers using offline methods.

> ➢ The first is using direct mail (letters, postcards etc. sent in the post to their homes).

> ➢ The second is by using newspaper advertising.

> ➢ The third is by using what's known as "guerrilla marketing" techniques.

At this point I should mention that local Radio can also be a very effective means of communicating to your potential audience, but it is significantly harder to get a great return on your investment than the 3 methods we're going to highlight... and we want to give you simple, effective strategies you can start implementing immediately.

How do I use direct mail?

Direct mail are letters and other mailings which are sent directly to customers' homes. According to the Direct Marketing Association, who are a global body for direct marketing, direct mail has a 600% outperformance compared to all digital channels. [6]

In other words you could get a six times better return on your money by spending it on direct mail, than you would by using any of the digital channels that are out there.

Direct mail is certainly a marketing method that should be

---

[6] https://www.iwco.com/blog/2017/01/20/direct-mail-response-rates-and-2016-dma-report/

considered and used - so how can it be used effectively?

The method I recommend to you is to send offers by letter. For example, this could be a Valentine's offer or any of the food holidays that are out there.

Your letter will use the same kind of structure that we've talked about previously: give a headline, make an offer, set a deadline, and include a tracking code so that you can measure performance.

You also might want to consider sending "lumpy mail", where you actually add a little gift inside the envelope. The gift might be a lollipop, a toy soldier, or something small along those lines which you can then make relevant to the offer you're giving.

So for example if you're putting a toy soldier in there, your headline might say "Shoot me down if this isn't a great offer!" which makes it clear why you've included the toy soldier.

The reason to use lumpy mail is that you want people to bother to open the letter – open rates for lumpy mail are typically higher than for traditional letters, because people are more likely to be curious and open the letter if it looks like there is an object inside.

Other techniques for increasing your open rate are to hand-write the envelope, and to put a postage stamp on them (as opposed to using a franking machine).

By using a headline which ties in with a free gift, there is an increased chance that the rest of your letter will be read and therefore responded to.

You may be wondering what to do if you haven't already got a customer base? How do you get a list of people to send the letters to?

There are companies out there who provide (for a cost) lists of people living in your area. When you buy these lists, it's wise to target people within the 8km (5 mile) radius we discussed earlier, and also to narrow down your target demographics.   I recommend looking at the age range of people on the list, and perhaps the affluence level as well.

For example if you're a high end restaurant it might not be effective to send letters to people who have a very low household income – you're more likely to have success with a list of people with more disposable income.

Similarly speaking if you're looking at sending promotions for people's birthdays, you could ask your list provider for a list of people within 8km of your restaurant, who are married and whose spouse's birthday is coming up in the next two to four weeks. You could then send them a letter saying something like: "Here's a great offer for your wife's birthday on XYZ date! We'd love to invite you to come and eat in our restaurant, and as it's her birthday, why not have dessert on us?"

In order to find companies that provide these lists go to Google and type in "consumer mailing lists" you'll get a list of possible businesses to work with. When you contact them, tell them exactly what you want (based on the kind of customer you want to market to) and they will then go and build you a list and tell you:

- ➢ How many people there are
- ➢ How much the list will cost you

Quite a few of these companies will also offer fulfillment for you as well. This means that if you provide them a letter template, they will do the printing and mailing for (often for a lot less than it would cost you to send).

Hopefully you can see how direct mail has the potential to be incredibly powerful: unlike the internet where a potential customer is bombarded with messages at any given time, when a person has found a quiet moment to look through their mail they might only have one or two letters.

If you combine all the techniques I've just described, then a hand-written, hand-stamped envelope with something "lumpy" inside it plus a great personalised offer is going to get their undivided attention and make it much more likely that they will consume what you're saying.

DIRECT MAIL

* Send an offer
* Try "lumpy mail"
* Use targeting to narrow your list
* Track the outcome by using an offer code

What is the right way to do newspaper advertising?

It's very easy to do newspaper advertising in the wrong way and burn your money. The number one thing you need to do is go local and ignore nationals.

As a business owner, I often get messages from companies offering me advertising in national magazines or national newspapers for what they deem a really reasonable price. But as a restaurant there's zero benefit in that whatsoever (unless you're a national chain) – if you're a typical restaurant and a local business then it only makes sense to advertise to local people.

Most towns, cities or boroughs have their own local papers or community magazines. The first kind of advert you can place is the conventional type, with a variety of different ad sizes you can opt for.

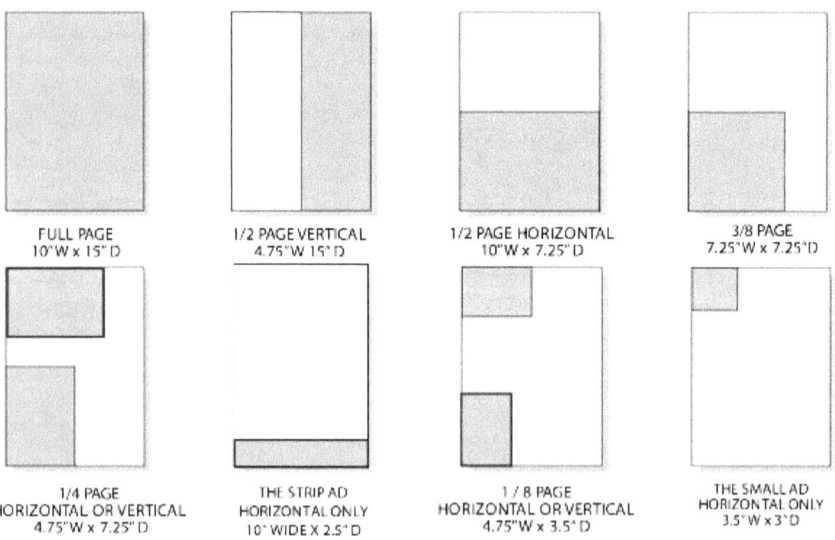

The rules for writing these ads well are just the same as they are for your Facebook ads, Google ads, or for any of the other ads that we have talked about. To recap, those rules are:

- ➤ include a headline,
- ➤ ive an offer or a call to action,
- ➤ have a deadline and
- ➤ include some kind of unique code that you can use to track the success of your advert.

In this case, because we are offline there is an additional requirement for your newspaper advert:

- ➤ state a way (or ways) for customers to respond to you.

When you're advertising online it's very easy for people to respond - they just need to click. Offline, however, when they're looking at your newspaper ad, if you forget to put an address or phone number in there then you might as well have not bothered with the advert. You need to ensure that you give some kind of contact information: a website, an address, your phone number (it just depends on how you want customers to respond).

State clearly how you want people to respond to the advert, by saying something like "To redeem this great offer, visit us and quote this code".

Now, there's a second type of ad which is without doubt the most effective kind of newspaper advert that you can have: an advertorial. You may well have seen this before in newspapers, where you're reading a news article and suddenly you realise what you're reading is not actually an article, it's selling something.

This what we call native advertising - it sits within the body of the newspaper, but it looks like it should be there.

Whereas adverts look like they're there to advertise, an advertorial looks like a story.

An advertorial should read like a news piece. It should tell an interesting story, talk about how amazing your food is, and then (as always) make an offer, have a call to action, give a deadline, have a tracking code and give several ways to respond.

Advertorials are larger than standard adverts, giving you more room to put across your message and give several ways for people to respond, depending on their preference. However this does mean that advertorials are going to be more expensive.

A further point to bear in mind is that some papers don't allow advertorials, so it's worth checking which local papers

---

[7] http://www.agoracosmopolitan.com/news/business/2011/12/11/2169-business-marketing-10-tips-to-craft-an-effective-advertorial.html

or magazines will run your ad.

With all marketing efforts you need to test what works, so first of all test the waters with a smaller advert, then if you're getting some response with that test a bigger advert. I do suggest that if you want to try and get the best response possible, move into an advertorial and test it.

NEWSPAPERS

* Make sure to structure your Advert correctly
* Include contact detail
* Try an advertorial

What is guerrilla restaurant marketing and can I use it in my restaurant?

Guerrilla marketing was a phrase coined by Jay Conrad Levinson, and it means marketing for little or zero cost in a creative way. A few examples are using external signage, window signage, human billboards or car signage.

A Boards

An example of external signage is having an A-board outside your restaurant with an offer on it. The A-board message shouldn't be just "We serve amazing food!" you want to give people a solid reason to come inside.

Passers-by are not necessarily going to believe that your food is amazing, they need to be compelled to come in and find out.

You might offer lunchtime specials, and the term "specials" is a good option because it implies a reduction in price, but doesn't necessarily mean you are reducing your price. So if you are averse to offering any kind of discount or financial incentive, then use the word "specials".

If you are happy to offer a discount then shout about it. People love anything that's free, and pudding (dessert) is typically one of the lowest costs things for us to produce, so go for a pudding. We know that a pint of coke costs us pennies or cents, so why not offer a free soft drink to get that additional custom in through the door?

Before you purchase or site an A-board, it's essential to check with your local council or authority whether they are allowed in your area, and whether you need to meet any conditions or seek any permissions. Many councils do not allow A-boards at all, whereas others allow them under certain circumstances.

Hanging Sign

Another example of an external signage opportunity is to have a hanging sign on your premises, in addition to the standard flat sign on the front of the building.

A sign hanging at a right angle to the building is can catch the attention of people walking down the street, without requiring them to turn and look at the restaurant frontage. Again, be sure to make an offer or give a call to action, rather than just stating your restaurant name. If you can't fit a call to action on, then let them know what food to expect... but please tell them something other than just who you are!

Hanging signs are another area where you should double-check permissions before you go ahead. Here in the UK, the government guidance suggests that hanging signs for restaurants are generally fine, providing they meet certain conditions (read through https://www.gov.uk/government/uploads/system/uploads /attachment_data/file/11499/326679.pdf - particularly Class 5), but it's best to double-check with your local planning authority whether you're in the UK or elsewhere.

Window Signage

Moving on to window signage, a lot of restaurants put signage up in their windows but typically it's non-promotional.

I strongly recommend that if you have window space that you can use, dedicate it to marketing material. Again, make an offer and if possible make it day specific (a different offer on Monday, Tuesday, Wednesday etc.). An offer holds more power of persuasion when there is a sense of it being limited or scarce – if a passer-by sees an offer which is only available *today*, there is more reason to take it up immediately versus an offer which appears to be ongoing.

One idea is to get yourself a chalk board and change you offer daily (or just have fun with it!). This way you don't have to pay for expensive window signage, you can vary your offer as often as you like, and they often look great in a window.

Another kind of signage you might consider putting up is a TripAdvisor sticker. You can request on free here: https://www.tripadvisor.co.uk/TripAdvisorInsights/n572/request-free-tripadvisor-sticker

As they are such a trusted site for restaurant reviews this can help you get a bump in customers walking past.

Human Billboards

Human billboards (also known as human directional, adwalkers or sign walkers) are another guerrilla marketing idea, and one that you see more of in the US than you do in the UK.

This involves employing somebody to stand in the street and advertise your restaurant by wearing a costume, printed T-shirt or perhaps a sign. Although - in the UK at least – you need a license to be able to hand out flyers, think creatively about alternative ways to get your message out there.

Do you have a product which could be offered for sample tastings?

If you serve the best coffee in your local area, why not take to the streets with a 5 litre insulated flask and hand out shot-sized samples?

If you serve a mean carrot cake, could you distribute bite-sized chunks to passers-by? Tell people to hand in their napkin at your restaurant today to get 10% off their bill all month – you'll then be able to track the success of your promotional activity.

To maximise success, incentivise your adwalker by giving them a bonus according to how many covers they bring in to the restaurant.

As with all things, check with your local authority regarding any regulations you need to be aware of, especially regarding signage and food/drink samples.

Car Stickers

The final guerrilla technique I'm going to suggest here is car stickers. A lot of businesses make the mistake of mounting the signage on the side of the vehicle, but this can be a wasted opportunity: the side of a car zips past you in a split second. The back of the car or the rear window is the best position for your signage.

We spend a lot of time at traffic lights or stuck in jams - if the car in front has an offer on it for a nice restaurant in the local area, you may well take it up.

I'm not claiming that this is going to give you a massive uplift, but it's very low cost so why not try it. If you achieve some results with your own car, expand the idea: you could pay people £10 or £20 a month to have your sticker on the back of their car (many people would take you up on the offer as it doesn't require any effort on their part).

The key point I want to communicate is that, wherever you have the opportunity for a potential customer to see something about your business, you should be giving them a reason why they should come into your restaurant.

GUERILLA MARKETING

* Creative + low or no cost
* Consider A-boards & hanging signs
* Use window signage to make an offer
* Try human adwalkers & car signage

PAGE INTENTIONALLY LEFT BLANK

CHAPTER FIVE
Returning Customers

How can I get customers to keep coming back?

Firstly, in order to keep your customers coming back for more, I'm going to assume that you offer great food and great service. It stands to reason that without those two things, nothing else you do will bring customers back for more. So with that assumption in place, there are three things you need to do to bring customers back to you more often. You need to:

- ✓ Capture their information
- ✓ Keep in touch with them
- ✓ Offer them incentives and reasons to come back to you

What's the best way to capture customer information?

You have two main opportunities to capture your customers' information, and the first is when they book.

This is where the value of online booking extends beyond customer convenience: when the customer is making an online booking, you are able to easily request consent to use the details they are providing (name, email address, telephone number and perhaps postal address) for future marketing purposes.

We have all become very used to ticking and unticking boxes when we fill in a form online, so your request to send them great deals and perhaps a birthday surprise, should not cause your newly found customer stress or ill-will.

With a telephone booking, your opportunity is limited. If they have called to make a table reservation, and you have asked for their name and phone number, those details have been requested for the purpose of making their booking. You are not legally allowed to go on to use those details for marketing purposes unless you get their specific consent.

It's one thing having a tick-box on a booking form online, but quite another asking your new customer over the phone (before they have even eaten with you) "Would you like to receive our special offers via text and email?". A phone call is a personal one-on-one interaction, and this is not the warmest start to their new relationship with your restaurant.

Your second opportunity to collect customer details comes after they have finished their meal. You have already had a chance to make a great impression; for your staff to come across as warm, human and trustworthy; to impress with your restaurant's great food and ambience; to make a connection. There should now be a good relationship to build upon, so you are better placed to be requesting details like birthdays and home addresses, and to ask permission to send offers and news.

I would recommend creating a simple paper form which your waiter or waitress presents towards the end of the meal.

He or she says something like:

"I hope you've all enjoyed yourselves this evening! If you don't mind popping down a couple of details here we'd love to send you some great offers and a special surprise when your birthday comes round. There's also a discount there for 10% off your bill here today (or "all your soft drinks free today", or any other low-cost bonus you can think of)".

You aren't requiring them to give their details, or making it *a condition* of getting 10% off, but what you are doing is encouraging a phenomenon called reciprocity.

Essentially, reciprocity is an unspoken social rule which we all feel compelled by, which means that if someone does something nice for you, you feel the urge to do something nice back for them.

The surprise 10% off discount puts in place the urge to do what you've kindly requested (fill out some details) and it also acts as proof that you'll be true to your word (sending offers and special surprises).

Provide enough forms and pens so that everyone at the table has the chance to easily give their details, and you have turned a potentially one-time visit into an opportunity to bring these customers back time and time again.

You are accepting a small upfront cost now, in order to profit more in the long term.

However, if you don't want to offer any kind of incentive, that's fine. You will still get people filling in their details if they have enjoyed the experience (although probably not quite as many). Just make sure to give them a really good "reason why" you are collecting information (the offer of good things to come in the future).

On the next page you can see an example of customer capture form we built for one of our clients (branded to our business for the purposes of this book).

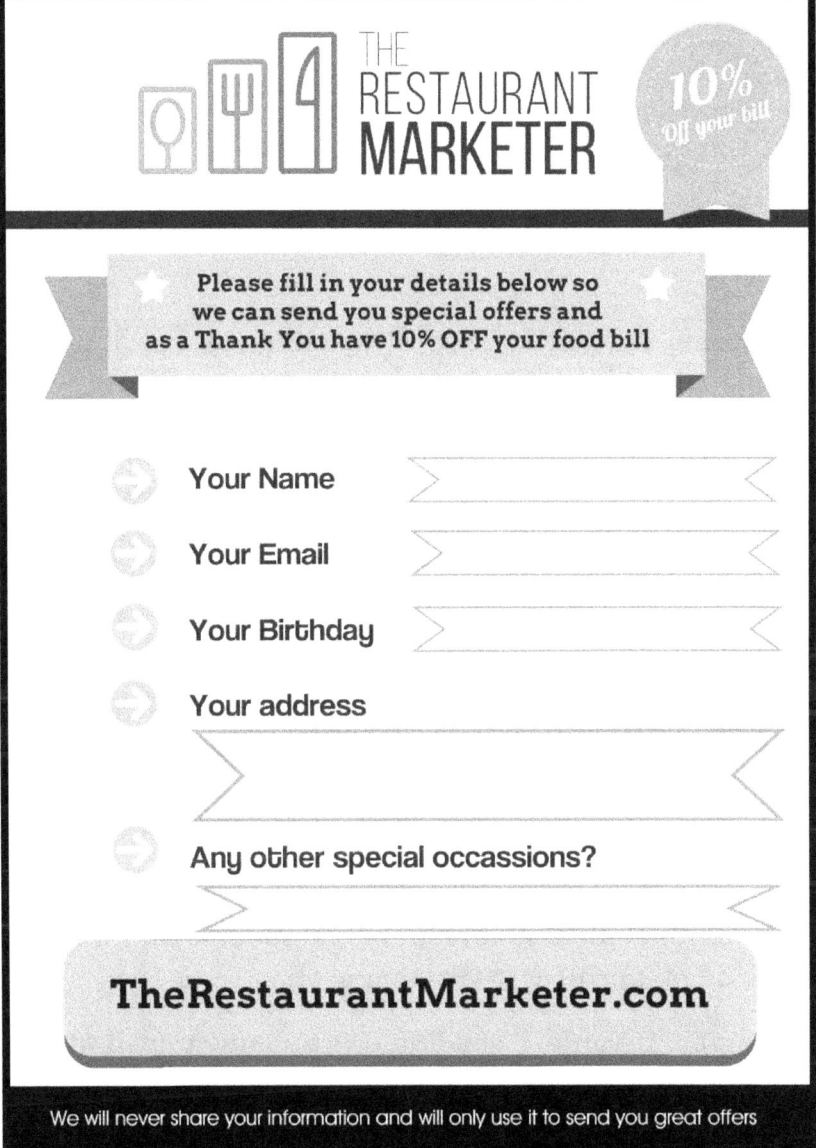

How do I keep in touch with my customers?

There are a couple of way to keep in contact with your customers:

- ➢ Newsletters
- ➢ Offers

Newsletters

You're going to want to send these either by email or post. It's up to you how regularly to send them, but I would recommend aiming for monthly.

Postal newsletters can be a good way of creating a community around your restaurant and, as we discussed earlier, are likely to have a higher open rate. However the downside is that they are higher cost than sending email newsletters.

The contents of a newsletter are similar to what we discussed putting on your Facebook page: include some entertaining local news, and perhaps something interesting about yourself or one of your staff members (because we're trying to create a sense of community).

You could also include a meal of the month, and mention some kind of incentive to visit you soon.

For example if you are sending out a newsletter in March, you could say "Throughout April we've got our Easter special - free Easter egg for your child" or something similar to incentivise people to choose your restaurant over your competition.

Obviously, make sure that you choose an incentive which suits your establishment - if you're a fine dining establishment which doesn't encourage young children then an Easter egg offer is not for you!

Offers and Incentives

Your second option for keeping in touch with customers is simply to send out a single offer, incentive or reason to come back to you.

If you are unwilling to go down the route of offering a discount, you can tell them about your new dish, new menu or new local supplier. Your offer can be sent by post, email or SMS.

SMS is text messaging, and it's not something which is often used by local businesses, but it's incredibly effective: 98% of SMS messages are opened by the recipient[8], whereas 21.17% of emails ever get opened[9].

Providing you have a well-structured SMS message (i.e.: including a headline, offer/call to action and deadline) the response rate can be excellent, and they are very inexpensive costing 2-4 pence (6 cents) per message to send out. Sending out 100 SMS messages may only cost you a few pounds or dollars, so you don't need a lot of responses in order to make a return on your investment.

SMS can be a highly cost effective way of marketing to your customer list.

---

[8] https://blogs.adobe.com/digitalmarketing/campaign-management/marketing-with-98-percent-read-rate-and-10-more-compelling-stats/
[9] https://mailchimp.com/resources/research/email-marketing-benchmarks/

What offers and incentives can I give customers to come back?

The answer to this question is limited only by your own imagination.

You can offer incentives related to customers' birthdays, public holidays such as Valentine's day and Mothers' Day, or even food holidays (there's a food holiday for every single day of the year, for example National Chocolate Day, National Bagel Day, National Doughnut Day).

Another option is to create special events: maybe you've got a wine tasting evening planned, or a Meet the Chef evening. You could even find an opportunity to make your customers feel part of the family, for example your daughter's graduation is coming up and you're really proud of that, so you plan a special event for her graduation day.

You could come up with dozens of reasons to have a special offer, deal or event for any particular day of the year.

And remember your offer does not have be an actual discount as long as the customer is getting a high perceived value. You could try a set meal with a glass of wine for a set price. As long as you work out you margins beforehand this can be very effective (and more importantly very profitable!).

GAINING REPEAT CUSTOM

* *Capture customer details during online booking &*
     at the end of the meal
* *Send monthly newsletters*
* *Create regular offers and incentives*

CHAPTER SIX – Customer Referrals

How can I get my customers to recommend me?

According to Nielsen, 92% of consumers trust recommendations from friends and family.[10] This means that recommendations can be a very powerful tool in your marketing mix.

You probably know that in order to get customer referrals, you need to ask for them. But there is a wrong way to ask for referrals ("You enjoyed your meal? Great! Please do tell your friends about us") and a right way, which I will explain shortly.

By requesting referrals in the right way vs. the wrong way you could boost them from maybe one or two referrals a month, to perhaps 20 or 30, turning them into your own personal marketing machine.

What's the right way to ask for referrals?

Firstly, don't assume that a referral will come – regardless how amazing the food and service were, assume that the customer isn't going to refer you even if you have asked them to. (As is the case with gaining repeat customers, I'm working on the assumption that your food and service is great, so there's every reason why your customers should tell all their friend and family about you.)

What I recommend doing is offering some kind of incentive or reward for your customers to refer somebody to you. These incentives could be an experience, a free meal, a

---

[10] http://www.nielsen.com/us/en/insights/reports/2012/global-trust-in-advertising-and-brand-messages.html

product of some sort – the options are endless.

The reason we want to actually offer our customers something in return for a recommendation is based on our old friend "reciprocity" which we discussed previously.

When someone has a great dining experience, they pay for this and the balance of "you did something great for me, now I'll return the favour" is typically satisfied. However if you then introduce the idea of rewards for recommending people, they feel this is fair trade (their time and recommendation for some sort of payment).

The psychology behind this is very powerful, and very effective. It's why loyalty cards work so well, and all we're doing is flipping this strategy and turning it into a referral program.

How do I create a referral program?

In order to have an effective referral program, you need to be able to track each customer who is referring new business to you.

To achieve this, when you ask a customer to refer people, you will take note of their contact details and give them unique code.

One method of doing this is to provide the customer with some mini cards or notes printed with their unique code, which they can hand to friends or family.

In addition to bearing the referrer's code, the card is also a voucher which the recipient can bring along to their first meal and receive a free dessert, side dish or soft drink (or whatever incentive you can think of that fits in with your restaurant).

When you receive the referral card you are then able to track the booking back to the original referrer using the unique code.

The method I have just described is, in my opinion, the quickest and easiest way for you to set up a referral scheme. There are websites online that help you manage the process, but these will typically charge you a set-up fee and amount per referral. They might be appropriate as you grow your referral business, but are not essential to start off with.

To keep momentum going in your referrers' mind, I suggest that you send them a letter or email on a monthly basis letting them know how they are doing.

Let them know how many people they've referred and whether they have done enough to redeem a small reward, or suggest that they keep working towards a larger reward.

You might also want to create a special prize for "Referrer of the Month", further incentivising your referrers by offering a higher value reward such as a free iPad.

CHAPTER SEVEN – Your Marketing Plan

I'm very busy – how long will all this marketing take me to do?

There's no doubt you will have to spend some time on your marketing, but as I said back in the first chapter: this is about working smarter, not harder. I'm sure you are already devoting some time to marketing activities, but perhaps you have identified some ideas in this book which might yield better results for the same time investment?

If you aren't devoting any time to marketing activities at the moment, then that *has to change* if you're going to reach your goal of getting new customers, and getting existing customers to return.

There are actions you can take to make marketing your business quicker and easier. Those actions are:

- ➢ creating an effective marketing strategy;
- ➢ automating certain parts of the process;
- ➢ and outsourcing certain elements of your marketing strategy.

How do I create an effective marketing strategy that won't take hours a day?

The first thing I want you to do is have a look at where your restaurant currently is, and then I want you to look at where you want to be and work backwards.

What I mean by this is, let's look at how many covers you're getting in each day of the week, and how many covers you're getting each month of the year, and then look at where you want to be to actually have the business you really want to have, and have the success and the financial freedom that you really want to have within your restaurant.

Plug those numbers in, and then we start to work backwards.

Say you're currently getting 20 covers in on a Monday and you want to get 40 covers in on a Monday, then you want to work backwards from that. You now know that you want to grow Monday night by 20 covers, and in order to do this you need to get some marketing assets working for you.

Ask yourself whether you have all the assets we have discussed so far in this book, and are they set up correctly? Do you have a Google my business page, do you have a Facebook page and a Facebook advertising campaign running, do you have a Google PPC campaign running, is your website set up correctly, are you using direct marketing, are you using signage to maximum effect, are you using any other tactics that we've discussed in this book?

If the answer to any of these questions is "No", then make a list of what you are missing.

The next step is to write yourself a plan of what you haven't done, and start to implement them, one at a time until your hit your target consistently.

Right away, I suggest that you start capturing your customers' information at the end of their meal. That is a step that you can take straight away – you really just need a printer, some paper and pens and to let your front of house staff what you need them to do.

At the same time, get your website in order to maximize the chance of new visitors choosing you above your competition.

After that, I recommend that you start off your marketing plan with paid online advertising (if you're not already doing it): get your Google PPC account set up, begin some Facebook advertising, and start marketing to people directly around you.

Once you've accomplished that task, move on to direct mail, followed by guerrilla strategies, and then move into customer referral programmes.

If you take action on all of these strategies in a structured and methodical way (and you're running a great establishment) then your business will grow and you will be able to achieve you revenue goals.

Is there any way to automate any of my marketing?

There are some aspects of your marketing strategy that you can automate quite easily. The main thing that can be automated is your email campaigns.

There's a variety of software available, but personally I recommend Active Campaign (http://www.activecampaign.com/).

Automation software allows you to enter your customers' information, and then send out marketing campaigns on autopilot.

For example, with Active Campaign you can add a Valentine's Day campaign that will be the same each year – you can set it to be automatically sent out three weeks before Valentine's day, with a Valentine's offer.

You can apply the same technique to your customers' birthdays – you can create a generic birthday offer that you send out to all customers two weeks before their birthday.

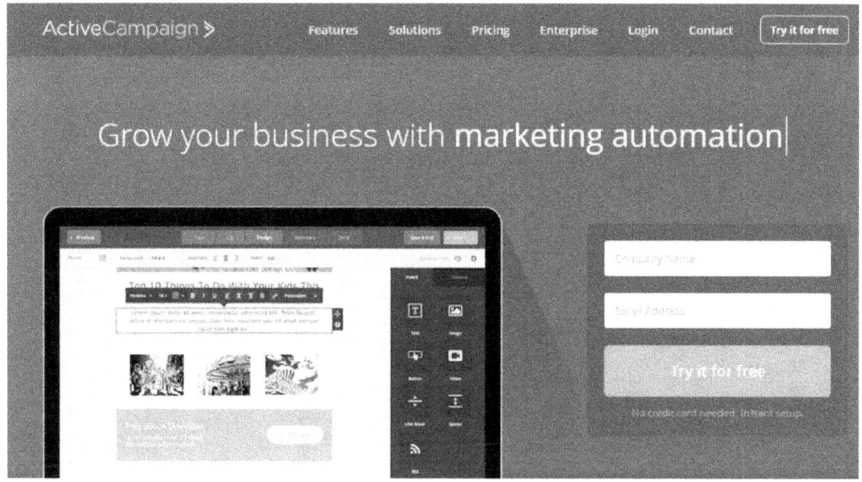

Your social media activity can also be automated: one of the most important requirements for success with social media is keeping up to date and active, but you also need to keep an eye on whether anyone is saying anything about you on social media.

There are various tools out there which can automate the process of achieving both of these aims – the one I recommend is Hootsuite.

Hootsuite lets you manage your Facebook, Twitter and YouTube channels all in one place; alerts you if anyone's talking about you and allows you to automatically post on your pages.

One of the things I really like about it is that while you're surfing the web if you come across any interesting story or website, you can click a button to post the story on your social media. They are automatically posted onto your Facebook page or Twitter account, taking out all the legwork for you.

I thoroughly recommend it because it takes hours a week off the amount of work I would otherwise have to do.

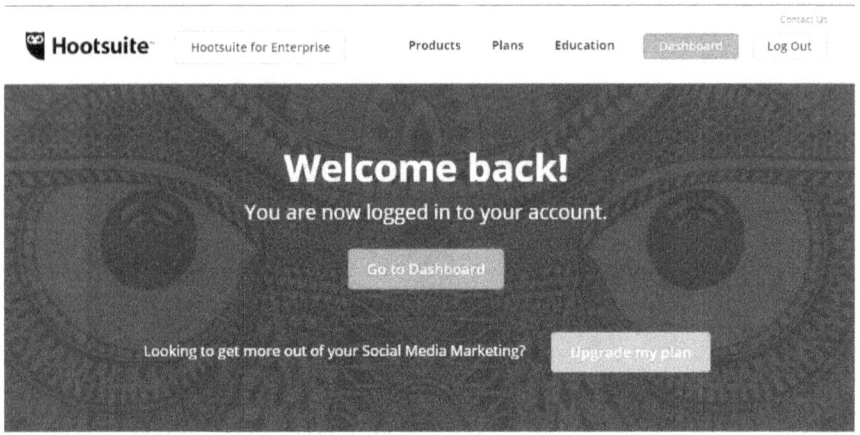

How do I outsource my marketing?

Outsourcing can be tricky if you haven't done it before, and I must say that it's not something I would recommend going into without thinking.

There are a few websites through which you can outsource your marketing functions, and the two that I would recommend are People Per Hour and Fiverr.

PeoplePerHour

Freelancers on People Per Hour (https://www.peopleperhour.com/) offer their services to you in fixed price projects called "Hourlies".

For example, you might pay somebody to write all your social media posts for the next month, write a new press release for your restaurant, redesign your menu or set up your pay per click campaign.

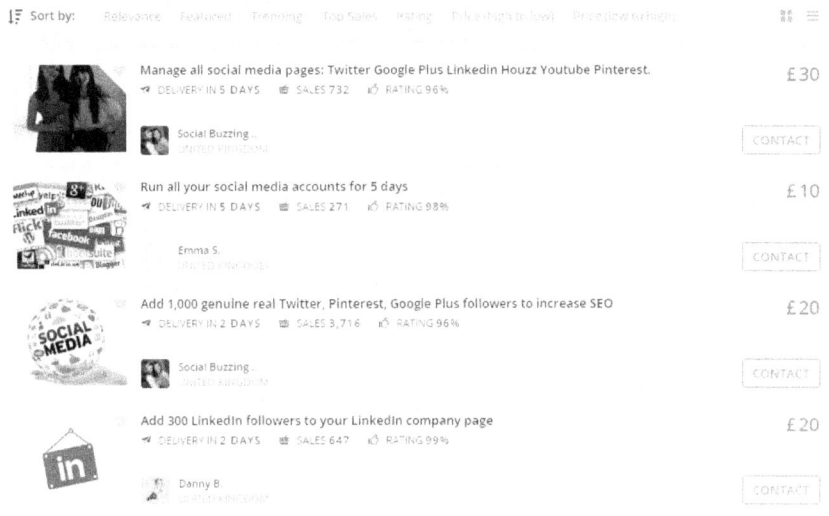

Any part of your marketing process can be outsourced to freelancers. However before you go ahead and outsource make sure that you look at the freelancer's reviews, ask them for examples of their work, and make sure that their work is in line with what you want and how you want to do business.

I have spent countless pounds and dollars on people who, at first sight and without checking them thoroughly, have turned out to be an absolute waste of time and money. In fact, in the past I have wasted thousands on unsatisfactory outsourcing, so it's really important to double check and then triple check before you hire anyone, to make sure you're going to get the best quality.

Don't just trust reviews, ask for samples of the work, *check* the samples of work, and only if you are still happy should you consider proceeding.

Fiverr

Fiverr (https://www.fiverr.com/) is a website where people will do almost anything for $5. It's a great site and you can get some really cool projects completed there.

If you move into the realms of YouTube retargeting (which we touched on in Chapter Three), Fiverr would be an ideal place to get some ads made. My wife did a promotion recently for one of the companies she works with, where she commissioned a video of people skydiving out of a plane and the skydivers then formed the logo of the company that they were marketing to. The basic video cost $5, and she paid a bit more for some extras such as HD and fast-track delivery.

As you can imagine, for that price the video was created using CGI but it looked totally real. So there is a lot that can be done through Fiverr, from a promotional point of view, which is almost guerrilla in tactics because it's so cheap and unusual.

What I don't recommend using Fiverr for is a Pay Per Click campaign, your Facebook advertising or something similarly significant, because you are simply not going to get a good service for that money.

In a nutshell, Fiverr is great for guerrilla marketing tactics and cool promotional ideas, but otherwise go for People Per Hour if you want to outsource.

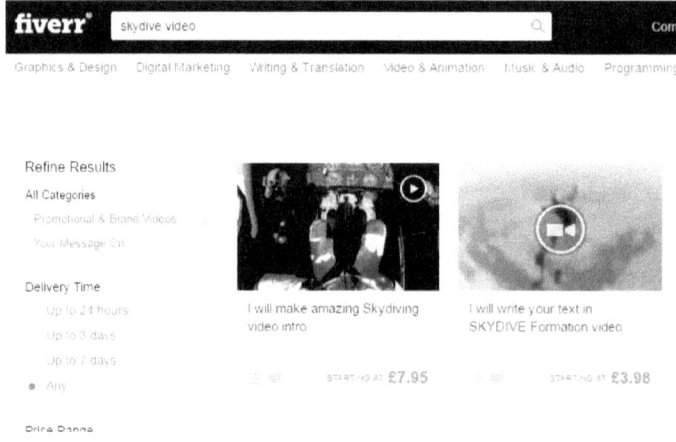

TIME-SAVING TIPS

* Create a marketing plan
* Take it step by step
* Automate your email campaigns
* Automate your social media
* Outsource (carefully)

.

FINAL THOUGHTS

I hope you've enjoyed reading this guide to marketing your restaurant as much I did creating it.

Although marketing your restaurant might, at first, seem like a daunting task it can be easily broken down into logical steps:

1. Make sure you website is as user friendly and inviting as possible

2. Get all your "free" online properties working for you

3. Use effective, targeted online advertising to bring in new customers

4. Use effective, targeted offline advertising to bring in new and back existing customers

5. Capture customer information once they're in your restaurant (or online when booking)

6. Keep in touch with your customers and give them a reason to come back

7. Create an effective referral program to get your customers marketing your restaurant for you

Steps 1 through 4 are mostly about getting new customers, and this is actually the more labour and cost intensive part of the process. Steps 5 through 7 are where the real money lies, and actually require a lot less work on your part (which is why the chapters where significantly shorter – the process is simple!)

So now it lies with you to evaluate where you currently are, then plug any holes you currently have.

I wish you every success with your marketing and if you have any questions, please get in touch with me through my website:

www.TheRestaurantMarketer.com

PAGE INTENTIONALLY LEFT BLANK